THE EIGHTH MOUNTAIN POETRY PRIZE

THE EIGHTH MOUNTAIN POETRY PRIZE was established in 1988 in honor of the poets whose words envision and sustain the feminist movement, and in recognition of the major role played by women poets in creating the literature of their time. Women poets world-wide are invited to participate. One manuscript is selected by a poet of national reputation. Beginning in 1993, the contest will be held on a biennial basis, in the even-numbered years. Publication and an advance of one thousand dollars are funded by a private donor. *Between the Sea and Home* was selected by Linda Hogan to be the 1992 winner of the Eighth Mountain Poetry Prize.

1989
The Eating Hill
Karen Mitchell
SELECTED BY AUDRE LORDE

1990
Fear of Subways
Maureen Seaton
SELECTED BY MARILYN HACKER

1991
Cultivating Excess
Lori Anderson
SELECTED BY JUDY GRAHN

BETWEEN THE SEA AND HOME

BETWEEN the SEA and HOME

Almitra David

THE EIGHTH MOUNTAIN PRESS
PORTLAND · OREGON · 1993

Grateful acknowledgment is made for permission to quote from:
"Reprise" from *Loba* by Diane di Prima, copyright © 1978 by
Diane di Prima. Reprinted by permission of Diane di Prima and
Wingbow Press.
"Resurrection of the Right Side" from *The Gates* by Muriel
Rukeyser, copyright © 1976 by Muriel Rukeyser, reprinted in *Out
of Silence: Selected Poems*, edited by Kate Daniels. Reprinted by
permission of William L. Rukeyser and TriQuarterly Books.
"Namaste" from *Soie Sauvage* by Olga Broumas, copyright © 1979
by Olga Broumas. Reprinted by permission of Copper Canyon
Press, PO Box 271, Port Townsend, WA 98368.

Cover art by Rochelle Toner, used by permission of the artist
Cover design by Marcia Barrentine
Book design by Ruth Gundle

First American Edition, 1993
2 3 4 5 6 7 8 9
Printed in the United States

LIBRARY OF CONGRESS
CATALOGING-IN-PUBLICATION DATA
David, Almitra, 1941-
    Between the sea and home / Almitra David. -- 1st American ed.
        p.   cm.
    ISBN 0-933377-23-1 : $21.95. -- ISBN 0-933377-22-3 (pbk.) : $10.95
    I. Title.
PS3554.A9147B48   1993
811'.54--dc20   93-7200

The Eighth Mountain Press
624 Southeast 29th Avenue
Portland, Oregon 97214
(503) 233-3936

ACKNOWLEDGMENTS

"Cathedral" was published in *American Poetry Review*; "Unburying Mother," "Notes from Delmira," and "Bag Lady: A Part of Her Poem" were published in *Beloit Poetry Journal*; "Kali-Durga" was published in *Long Pond Review*; "For Muriel Rukeyser" was printed in *Painted Bride Quarterly*; "Fig" was published in *Poets On*; "Prologue" and "House by the Sea" were published in *6ix*; "Medusa" was published in *13th Moon*.

A limited edition of "Annie Crow Road" was printed in portfolio form by Cathy Beard at Potter Press, Vermillion, South Dakota, 1988.

"Prophecy" and "Cathedral" were published as part of the chapbook *Building the Cathedral*, Slash & Burn Press, Philadelphia, Pennsylvania, 1986.

Acknowledgment is also made to the Pennsylvania Council on the Arts for two grants which enabled me to spend time on this manuscript, and to the Blue Mountain Center in New York, where many of these poems were completed.

"Under this temple there is a well so ancient
it will abide the mouldering of the floor.
This night, for healing, I'll tear up
the flagstones;"
　　　　　—Diane di Prima

CONTENTS

II. ANNIE CROW ROAD

III. BAG LADY: A PART OF HER POEM

IV. BETWEEN THE SEA AND HOME

Prologue

patience
has nothing to do with
my continuing

nothing to do with the
sea's constant
wearing at

what he calls
unchangeable   I unwrap
resin-soaked linens

free my hand to
write again   he thought
when he burned my letters

he thought
in Alexandria   that
would be the end of it

each time I have
come into his town
walked near his door

he has begun to
gather twigs for
the inevitable burning

remember   when he
goes to the well   when
he cups his hands

my words
surface with the
water in spring

I. Unburying Mother

Begin

begin with the cats because
that's how it is   the
howl of starvation
outside your window   begin

with the long wail that
you sometimes confuse with the
cry of a baby or a
wild thing dying

once you tried to
feed it   (your grandmother could
put out a saucer of milk and
not think twice)   you said

I will feed this one hungry thing

and when you set the
dish out a tongue went
through it
down   down under the
foundation of your house
and pulled it up to
the roof of a mouth
unfed for centuries

If She Is Fourteen

1

if she is fourteen
on the outskirts of
Winslow Arkansas and
the night is not
different from other
nights in which her father
holds her against the
ground or against the bed
against him   if she
has begun to bleed and
her father calls her
honey or whore and
the January wind makes
her unable to move as the
winter sap of the redbud
if she waits until April
and walks to the river and
wonders at the stirring
in her belly   if she

opens her hand and sees
nothing there to give
and thinks of stories of
the city   of wages   a
bed for herself   for
her child   if she
stands alone   woman alone
and imagines

a safe place

she will walk
keep to the edge of the road
sleep in the fields   move
through each day fed by her
idea
basic and revolutionary

2

it is a matter of prey
the woman said   *to*
live in a man's city
you need a dog

if she were a wildcat
she would leave her
child alone and
find meat
she would come back with
food from
an honest hunt

if she is fifteen and
the day is not different
from other days in the city
and she finds her baby
dead   its blood
in the dog's mouth

from what hunger
will she scream   whom
will she eat

Fig

in Italy the fig is
called the poor man's fruit
abundant   sweet
spread over the landscape

in Pittsburgh they can't buy
that kind of jam
not even the ones who've
worked in the mills a hundred years

they can't grow figs in their yard
I've seen them fooled
by the July sun   by the
half-melted tar in the streets
fooled into thinking it would
stay warm enough long enough

women still cut crosses
in their bread   still roll pasta
to dry on the table   still wait
for the orange zucchini blossom

they know where they are
they don't expect
to smell Mediterranean air
don't look under their pillows
their houses are brick
and if a rose blooms — *basta*
I think of Etruria
when grandmother mentions Rome

14

and when she says   God
I remember the one
of the Wild Fig Tree   the one
whose hands are like mine
She in whose house there is
sun enough for figs

Notes From Delmira

Delmira Agustini, 1886–1914, Uruguayan
poet, murdered by her husband whom she
had left after twenty-six days of marriage.
Her work includes the most erotic poetry
of the Latin American Modernists. This in
spite of her youth, her sex, and the very
sheltered circumstances of her life.

1

Do you think
because seventy years have
passed, or because you
eat your lunch without

pounding your fists,
that he would not put
a bullet through your head?
Do you imagine that
knowing me is not an

act of rebellion? Perhaps you
believe that your
clothes will save you. You have
not fought the fashion, you say.

Dear one, do you recall the
soft blue dress I wore when
I left him? I was an
angel in it.

16

2

I write to you as though
dialogue were a
possibility, as though we
might walk together through
Montevideo. In the

park I discuss Nietzsche with
myself. The mood here is
scientific, the talk is of
observable facts which do

not include you, and do not
include the women from
before the fire. I am
the woman in my room, writing

at night, writing while
demons claim my bed. I am
the woman in my room, bargaining
with Eros. I write from the
temples of Thessaly and Paphos.

To reappear becomes more
difficult. Each morning to
appear, dressed to
walk through this city as

though it were a
cathedral. I cover my
voice by day. It
passes easily through the
streets. These streets have

no ancient ruins, no
hint of the woman who said her
poem in a clear voice, who
spoke where the

cathedral stands now in
Plaza Matriz, and the
cafes fill up with
men's words.

Do you wonder
why I don't enter? Are
you shouting Claim a
table, order brandy, speak!

You see that my arm is
through my father's, my
step demure. Will your
stride be longer, your
walk freer? Dear one,

my voice waits for the
night. When Montevideo
awakens, my name eludes me,
the ancient root of
my name. I search for

a waterfall I climbed, for
what was given to me then,
before the forest split,
leaving me on this side.

3

The climate here is
temperate, never too
hot. The train to town is
comfortable. I ride
three times a week to

study French and piano.
What is language? What is
my language? If this
breeze came from the
Seine instead of the Plata,

could I read my poems by day?
A man here was shot for
an essay he wrote, using
"love" and "free" in the
same sentence. Could he have
said it in French? I
think of you,

your language, your music,
will you have found
your own by the time you
find me?

Last night I saw Sarah Bernhardt
be *La Sorciére*. I
saw her burn, saw
them burn that gypsy

wildwoman witch Sarah-Zoraya. I
sat still, crossed my ankles,

oh, dear one, there will
be no holding back
this fire. It burns in

my room when Erato comes, when
she takes me to her gardens
to the gods' feasts and
their struggle for her prize.

She visits me by night. She
knows my room, my old doll, the
flowers, the desk, the chair.
She knows where I wait for her.

But where am I now? Who is
this man who calls me wife,
and where shall I
wait for Erato? I have no

room here. For twenty-six
days I have looked for my
room in his house. It is not
here, my voice is not here.

You know that I
will leave him, that I
left him, that we shall
always leave him.

4

After he's broken them, the
horses wait for
food and water. They
nuzzle his pocket.

Now and then one
goes wild again, loud,
runs for that stream
he has called mythical.

He will come after me
with his gun. He will
call it love, you know that.
He will say I have
written of passion, of

Eros, of a garden that
he has not seen. You know
that he also loves trees,
that he dreams of bringing the
eucalyptus under his roof.

Do you think
because seventy years have
passed, or because he
killed himself,

that he has finished?
Do you not
hear him
loading his gun.

5

I've not slept through
the wars. I don't
sleep while you work.
I watch you

piece fragments of an
ancient vessel,

make it useful again,
give it your own marks,
bring it

into your time. You remember
I wrote that people wear
gloves of ice, that they
fear the rush of their

blood. I write to you as
though dialogue were a
possibility, as though we
might walk together through

Plaza Matriz. Is the
numbness wearing off? Do
you hold a lusty daughter?
Are you beginning to feel
the century change?

The Line

she's trying to
vomit quietly   the
door closed
radio loud
window open to
December   the

air rushes straight to
her bones   as though
there were nothing
between her skeleton and
the wind   as though

the thick wool sweater
over her uniform
served only a
visual purpose   as though
it too had crossed over the
line between her
world before and now

nothing is left from
then   not the
nuns   school
her mother   her
room   she

can see them   she
sees them as clearly as
the pine green cable stitch

of her sweater   she
looks into the mirror
puts her hand on her stomach
waves begin again   why
nausea for the beginning of
a life she wonders   she

closes the window
opens the door to the
hall   hears the
house   late for

school her mother is
saying   breakfast her
mother is saying
the band   your
flute   a
Christmas concert   but

it must be
October   she
can see the red
leaves   the
homecoming game   the
party   if she

could speak she would
ask her mother what
month it is but
her voice is gone   she
last heard it in
October   loud   loud
but no one else
heard it then   no

one rushed to her
no one pulled him
away from her   now she

pulls at her
sweater   her
mother is asking her
what she would like
for Christmas

For Muriel Rukeyser

"the power of eyesight is very slowly arriving
in this late impossible daybreak
all the blue flowers open"
                    —Muriel Rukeyser

three flights you
climb   to this room
where windows don't
shut out October wind   you
stand   defying
the doctor who said
stay home   in this room
women come together to write

and again you have
come to the gates
this time   you say   to a
new power of women   to
the woman as writer
you have
survived wars to say this

outside   no
fireworks open the sky
this celebration is quiet as
our breath   you say   listen
to each pause   to
every drawing in and
letting go

when the rhythm of your breath was
broken   your voice
your balance
shattered as though
someone   (perhaps from a
battlefield you crossed)   shot at
your right side
you called it
lightning from behind the eyes

your eyes   this morning
see us   see
the structure of
this room   of
the trees nearly bare in
the wind   you
gesture as you speak
poems   you say
roll down my right arm

Unburying Mother

1

with only the tip of the spade
I probe
I am
afraid to push the earth
there is the possibility
of worms   I don't
want to cut flesh

when you rocked me
your fingers stroked
my forehead
I watch the earth
split
my fingers are white
gripping the spade
my fingers are
white as the flour on
your hands
kneading bread
you rubbed your hands together
I hear the gritty sound
this dirt is dry
there are webs of roots
I don't recognize
didn't ask
while you rolled out the pasta
or pinched the edges of the pie crust
I never asked what
was under the kitchen

2

my weight shifts
leg to leg
the veins in your legs
ink
spreading wordless
if I asked   you said
"only at night they throb"
when I reach you
I will massage your legs
you will tell me of
when you danced those
Saturdays you slipped
past your mother's bed
without her calling
Anna...Anna...
do you know Anna
if the morning star were
still called Ishtar-Inanna
no crucifix would have hung
on your bedroom wall
no selfless Mary would have
smiled at your self's death
Anna   how you would have danced

3

I've hit rock
pacienza   pacienza
you would say
nobody's born with it
not like feet arms eyes
pacienza
useful in prison

nuns call it a virtue
sometimes at night I think
I have it   I say
now that the sun has set
I have it
but my hair sticks out
and my clothes hang crooked

I'll move these
rocks with my hands
rocks heavier than
your two babies
dead after birth
heavy as the doctor
who would not cut
who said do it alone
you'll feel more like a woman
you'll feel more

now the earth
gives under me
the third time he relented
after all   it wasn't Abruzzi
it was Pittsburgh
and 1941 was modern
was softer than
the limestone that
never moves in Abruzzi
he relented   made
the incision like
god splitting a mountain
letting water rush
spilling over his hands
my head in his hands

4

now the sun warms
my shoulders
the digging is easier
you rubbed my back
asked was I
cold hungry tired sad
did I need
now I need
to tell you
when you left I was
in the middle of a sentence
my voice lost
in someone else's sound
like a pebble dropped
into someone else's sea
now I know
our words
the ones you hinted
with your eyes   your hands
I know our words
the ones you made into
bread for supper
the ones that never
spoke of your hunger
I feel the sun on
my shoulders   soon
we will eat together
we will have
coffee and warm anise bread
and the words will fall
from your apron
from your lips   your eyes
from your thick gray hair
loose and wild

the words will fall
and we will dance in them
and laugh and cry in them
hand in hand   two women
we will crumble our silence
like this dirt
relenting
beneath my feet

II. Annie Crow Road

Marsh

she walks across the
wood planks   across
this place where
land and water merge

womb uncurled
spread out   wet and
rich

water pushing up
earth settling
soft and fertile as
her own eggs

and as quiet

when the cattails
wave with the
wind from the bay
and the crane keeps
watch   and the
bees search   she

thinks she hears
beginnings   those

almost silent
separations of cells

Geese

when she hears them she
stops whatever she's doing
and looks up
sometimes their cry
pulls her off the
ground   carries her
over the fields and
south along the bay

she feels the wind
against her body then
and her wings

hunters place cardboard birds
around pits   they
paint beer cans yellow and
toss them like
ears of corn   eventually

a goose will fall for it

when she flies with them
she tries
to tell them this

Tiger Lilies

when the mist
and the sky and
the gulls are gray
and the heavy
wet air settles on
her shoulders and

she feels cold even
though it's June   she
walks along a back
road to the bay   stops
near the tiger lilies

she must do this
stand close to
Lilith's flower   begin
to feel warm again   as

though they were
flames   as though
breathing next to them
might satisfy that
deep longing for orange

Fishermen

usually their hunt is
well defined   their
nets measured   they
know the rules   the
time to begin   the
signal to end   they

know the tides and
currents   the depths
the rocks
what they fear are the
mood swings   the
tricks   the fury

there is no such thing as
a steady wind

on the good days   when
bushels fill with
rockfish and crabs
they don't mistake it
for a promise

those come later   after
they dock   slide
hands into pockets and
go for beer

Sailmaker

fifty years ago his
father taught him
the angles and
proportions
taught him to
cut straight and
sew a tight seam

he was fourteen then
dreamed of
running loose

now every day but Sunday
he climbs the
steps to his loft   to
his sewing machine and
bolts of canvas

everyday he comes to
grips with the wind

how to catch it and
make it useful

Mulberries

with the summer solstice
she's ready for
her first taste   the
sweet juice on her
tongue   she

knows where they grow
the back roads   the
paths along the bay where
the soil is
rich and deep   she

has watched their progress

timing is crucial   if
she sleeps too late   if
she wanders casually to
the bushes as though
there were no race

she'll hear no
apologies sung to her   just
full bird sounds
content
from the trees

Vultures

they are necessary   she
knows that

she knows
they can't hurt her   their
beaks are not
strong   designed to
tear flesh already dead

she watches them
soar   watches their
wide circling   they

can spot a carcass from
miles   and they

can see her heart
its measured
number of beats

Ruins

this should look like
death   the
house leaning   its
skeleton bare   the
grass growing high
through the
walls

and the car

the car in front
trapped in the act of
parking
held fast until
it too succumbed to the
wild green

this should make
her think of death
make her think twice
before opening her
basket   spreading
her blanket

can she sit on this
will she
hold everything back for
just a minute and
call it a picnic

Crows

sometimes at night she
tries to think of
new ways to
keep them away

what good is a
row of tin cans or
a straw man when
the trees explode black

she knows how they
come back and back
she hears them cry
hungry from Valhalla

and she's not ready to go
there's corn to grow and
horses to feed and
crabs to scoop from the bay

sometimes after supper
when the dusk hovers for
a minute before black she

sees thirteen Valkyries
waiting in the
oak tree outside
her bedroom window

Paths

not as the
crow flies   these

follow the earth   its
curves   its
ups and downs   they

run through the fields
crawl along the
edge of the bay   stretch
to clear the way to
mulberry bushes   they

are made of shells   she
wonders at this
amazed to walk over
shell-paths

connections almost
invisible   except
when the
moonlight catches them

Shells

she has photographs of
long-spined star shells
bubble shells   spindle shells
and abalones

these she has never
held in her hand

here she finds
what's left of
oysters   mostly
gray and brown
everyday patterns
basic as stew

still   she collects them

sets them on sills and
end tables and shelves
she likes to have them
with her in the
house   to
see them
in a different light

Crabs

she grew up
eating them   tossing
their shells onto
piles for compost   not

thinking of cycles

now she watches them
from the edge of
the dock   watches them
slide by
blue   iridescent

they will signal
the end

when all the planets are
in Cancer   the world will
dissolve   back
to elements   back to
the sea

she lowers her feet into
the water   feels the
undertow

III. Bag Lady: A Part of Her Poem

Bag Lady: A Part of Her Poem

just remember   I'm the one
who left I said
I will not touch your hand
or your ear or play little
circles on your neck   I
will not move on
your voice the way a gull
rides the air   its
wings still

I said I'm
going to my own
side of the
streetlights stars
broken glass dogs
wheels stuck in shit I
built this cart
myself

when the elevator
opened they wheeled my
mother out
melting in front of me as
though the sun had burned
through the hospital roof
look at my fingers if
you're not afraid honey
they've been in that pool

do you
think I should have cut
my fingers off   I
did in fact have one
amputated   the doctor
put it down to frostbite
now you accuse me of
friendlessness
I tell you I wouldn't
have walked out if
we had begun with colors   if
the lectures had been
orchid and chartreuse like
Empress Carlotta's rug   if
we had begun with oils
instead of charcoal

oh my hat
you appreciate the
wide purple of it   do you
wonder at its power to
stop you even here on
40th Street where you
rush clutching keys   are your
hands used to that tight grip

when your keys don't work   when
they don't hold back the
August fear that
breathes hot against your
door   will you
toss them   will you
book one only one
voyage   sea days

tea afternoons
cress sandwiches
strawberry tarts with Devonshire cream
will you decide to
be an actress at the Schubert
when the old woman in
Chelsea reads your face
will you believe her

I didn't want to know
of bombs in Spain   only
Lake Como   Carlotta's bedroom
guarded there as though I
would have stolen that
orchid   sold it
traded it for whatever you
think you want

here on 40th Street honey
what do you want
I had keys then too   you
know the big brass
ones for trunks filled with
dresses and scarves and
art books   I
like Watteau   the man playing

the violin under
trees   a man small in
the enormous forest
I think he was a
clown   dressed as
he was in my colors
in the woods   do you
like wood

do you like to
hold a piece of it and
run your hand over
the grain until there is
no more roughness   oh
I have been called tough
but I'd rather be called
resilient

what did he ever make of
wood   the man who
called himself carpenter and
said he loved me
after the hospital I
went with him
his asthma so bad
he couldn't breathe

we ate doughnuts and coffee and
his plans to build a house
he left in the rain with
his heavy breath
sometimes I check the
station but I'll tell
you this honey if a
train ever does come in

I hope
my mother's on it   I
have a ruby ring for her
and beads from the
woman of Xochimilco   her
prayer beads
healing beads she
holds to

keep sickness away   the
hospital had no color
there my carpenter built
his stories   my
mother will
come in September when the
leaves are
copper and orange

when the boys knock
over my cart and
laugh while they
steal I say
it's raining   it's lightning
it's an earthquake in Peru
it's a famine not far away
it's the wind let loose between skyscrapers

your raincoat is ugly honey
it's parched for color
like sand   you need a
purple sash   a scarf like
this one I'll sell you for
a dollar and here's an
embroidered drawstring pouch
you can carry your keys in the

way Japanese carry pearls
let's move on   two
hours here   two
hours in another place
are you afraid to
sit still   your
fingers on your knees
not holding   not

keeping cats or
birds alive   I know
how to wait and
I decide when
to move
mother says I will
be an actress if
I have discipline
do you have that
when you dress in the
morning do you have a
plan with hours and
weeks   does it
fit you
do you like its color
if you alter the

seams too often
edges come apart but
you can save remnants   this
sash is from a gown that
reached to the floor and
it's yours for
a dollar   you see I am
brilliant with remnants

I know what to do with
leftovers   my nightmare
is not the half-ruin
it is that clear day when
no adjusting will help
they will have finished
there will be nothing for
a quilt or a stew

listen
I'll recite my knitting piece

I want to
unravel what you've
done   pull
everything apart like
a badly knit scarf
unbuild your prisons
unbloody your battles
uninvent your schemes
oh   you lovers of
strategy   you players
with words and gun
you carriers of statistics

stand up

I want to
measure what is
here   and
what size you are

a lament is a long *oh*
oh   for the ghosts kissed
and the time spent to
make them real   *oh*
to blow out the candles
oh   like your eyes
when you saw your father
oh   open as the sores on my legs

close your eyes   look away
I'm still here   you're still
here   touch your leg   how

easily the skin would
open   how many years would
gush out   as though
you'd never tried to
hold them back   never
locked a door

I was watching the
Florentine sun glint off
marble muscles   I was
in a battlefield so stark I
had to close my eyes
I was under him
on my back   looking up
like a child searching the
clouds for a familiar face

have some blueberry muffin
I like them with more berries
old Clara gives me
one every Friday   Nick gives
me kabob on his good days
I buy my own coffee when
they let me in the store   when
I say let me in they look and
I'm too big for them

my hand   look at it honey
it won't sign papers for
bed and a bowl of soup
a fishbowl of fish   oh
the goldfish is really a
great green carp   a
loose wet scaly hungry
fish   too big to live
in a glass or a bag

or the hospital hallway
so white   so white
I cut myself to see the
color   to smell if
I was still there
honey why are you still here
what happened to your hurry
if I read your face
will you believe me

I believe in the
woman of Xochimilco and
blueberry muffins   this
small gold hand from a
Yucatan temple and
luck   *la buena fortuna*
what do you do to
keep devils away   your
keys won't work

oh let's sing about work   I
worked in Macy's not
fast enough to pay for
the theatre   I worked
in a bank a cafe and a
school not fast enough
to pay for theatre not
fast like your legs when
you rush along 40th Street

let's sing about work
outside in July   outside
in December on the
outside   on the sidewalk
hot   steam   ice   wind
snow in the wheels

push in the wind
when it rains I
could kill you

get the
fuck off my street
the night here is
mine   I
grab it with
both my hands   it
shakes me   I
hang on   it
pushes me to the
pavement   I
sleep with it   I
know how to
sleep hanging on
the night here is
mine   when it
crawls on my skin
I scratch
my blood comes   after
sunset I am
the color
I vomit   I cry
the night takes it all
it tries to
shake me   to
pick me off and
fling me over the
edge   I
hold on when the
edge is Xochimilco
I hold on when
it's 40th Street   I
hold on when the

rain is called Tlaloc
hold on through
all the nights of
the Wise Women   I
hold on while you
turn in your bed
seeing me in your sleep
seeing us both against
black
our colors the
only light   oh
run   run the
fuck off my street
the night here is
mine

or stay
watch the water with me
watch what
rises from the lake
and sleeps crumpled in
the doorway like that
tissue in your hand   do you
have an extra   my
nose is running

keep on running honey   how
long are your nights   how
long before morning
saves you with its
list of
things to do   to do
things   to do
them fast enough to
pay for the theatre
what do you do first in

the morning   I
piss in the street   water
to water   I
like that better than
dust to dust   if it's
a dusty day let's
have a beer
watch me part the

crowd   watch when I
walk to the bar and
spread my elbows   we'll
drink to another
dividing of the sea
and what will you find when
we go to the sea honey
what will you look for
do you know yet what
you've lost   have you felt
it next to you like the
absence of a lover   like
a ring with
gold prongs and
no stone   do you
remember what to
look for when we
go to the sea

and what will you bring
I love picnics honey   let's
make it a feast   bring
oranges   the kind from
Tampico   the kind that don't
fall apart   I know their
skins   I can tell

where they came from even
when I find them

against this curb   do you
doubt it   do you say
nothing because you're
hungry   or because you
are remembering the dead   why
are you walking away from
me honey   are you looking for
a curtain   something to
close   here   this cloth was

woven in Chimalpa   the
purple and green from
Carlotta's bedroom   hang it
across your window honey   you'll
need the color   you'll look for it
when the lake laps at your bed
and here's a bag to
keep your things in if the water
gets too high

IV. Between the Sea and Home

Prophecy

my grandmother came to
this place
and prayed
and brewed the
tea of acacia flowers
and spun the image of
Hecate's sphere   she
knelt and rocked and
said oh my daughter
they will cover your
body in black and
your face and your head
they will cover
and stones will be built
higher than trees
and they will sing only
to gods with no breasts
and with stones they
will kill you
when you love
and burn you
when you heal
and you too
will forget
Aradia's names

and you will forget how
to walk   how to breathe
and your voice will become
weak   as the

eyes of the salamanders
born into darkness

and you will chant only
the words of men
and when the strength of
your body and the vision of
your mind has been syphoned
you will give them your children
your breasts and your womb
they will own as their fields
and you will call your own
death   blessed

soon we will not
feel this holy ground
under our feet   only the
cold smoothness of their
carved stones
no circles open to the
sky   rings
wheels of the seasons
Sacred Womb

they build corners
closed to Her light
on the walls they draw
joyless faces   they
burn candles at the feet of
a woman with downcast eyes
a woman deaf to the
rage of Aradia inside her
a woman who does not avenge
the rape of her daughters
oh my daughter
they kneel at the corpse of

the Mother
and upon Her death
they build their church

Cathedral

make a window of
stained glass   not
too heavy   you need to
carry it with you

look through it

the altar can be
red or gold or
whatever you like

flash a rosette onto
a gray wall
glance across the pews
with blue-green
motion as though
the sea had
never left

now kneel   don't
drop the glass
look
even the floor seems
glorious

The One Who Kills Cats

the one who
kills cats in
alleys and empty lots
sometimes looks at
his hands   not on
purpose   it happens
when he pours catsup on
a sandwich or
grabs a beer   it
happens that his hands
pass in front of his
eyes   he

sees nothing un-
usual   no
scar from an
ancient claw   he
knows nothing of
nine lives
nine-fold goddess   he

doesn't remember that
night in Egypt when
the long sharp cry
awoke his neighbors   how
they chased him when
they saw the
dead cat   how they
killed him

Medusa

when first I heard the
hissing in my hair
I called it a laugh
and left it at that —
there was breakfast to be made

now the earth
lies hot
in the afternoon sun
I feel it against my back
lying here   face to the sky
I see
what is sprouting from my head

my fingers slide through
my hair   back to the
pond where I sat
pleased as the lilies   and knowing
back to that day when
my blood and
the stream and
the pond flowed together
I stood no smaller than
the mountain   my hair
moving with the clouds

in the dark you
stroke me and say how
smooth I am   how

there is nothing rough to
offend your hands

when this morning's sun
warmed the bed   my hair
moved on the pillow   you
saw me   the light
shining through my hair   you
came toward me and
stopped   stood
in front of me as
still as stone

Kali-Durga

the lion I ride is
hungry   you don't
want to see teeth
only at night you
call me   when
you lie sick
and your breath is
heavy as the
black air   you
want me to
chant away your
fever   to eat
your dark dream
and leave quietly

what do you
expect from this garden
here   where I
drop what you
give me   you
don't want to
find serpents and
skulls and

not silence   when I open
my mouth to
howl and scream
the trees bend
in a thousand storms

Even Though

even though it
was January   she
put her feet
into the Delaware
until they felt like
nothing

ice-cakes floating
seemed
smooth satin pillows

and you know how the
wind in winter can be a
howl or a cry   it's
hard to tell which

so that when she
laid her baby in the
river   she wasn't sure
if the cry came
from the trees   or
from the blanket
drifting
white

Avenue du Bois 23

for Renée Vivien

leaded glass is not enough
drapes thick
as thirty-two years
swallow flecks of light
that blunder like fireflies
into a Venus trap

Parisian air is dense
incense hangs on it
like tapestry
on a gray wall

you move
from desk to
chair to
window
a candle pacing
the edge of her grave
you slide
finally   fast
as gravel down
a barren hill
you slide

this room is limp   violet
my face opens to the sweet death
you arrange

your spring
you are burning
in front of me
and I can only
stand
there is no water here

you say
water is Mytilene
is olive groves
gone twenty-five centuries
you dreamed the charts you followed
your compass drawn
to an ancient sky
to a fragment of Sappho's song
and she would be there
the sea rocking at her feet
and she would braid her
flowers in your hair and you
would know her poems as your breath
and you would sing them to the sea
and she would wash the soot from your body
the caked
Parisian dust
this sky is
black drapes
one grave   black
the smoke that curls
near your desk
paper   you
write your
body
cell by
cell your poems
grow full   they

are grapes ripening in
the vineyards of Lesbos
your fingers
thin   white   each
day you
eat a little rice

you read
Verlaine and Baudelaire
and you are dead they say of
"le mal de fin de siècle"
they say
melancholy is:

and they write
with their windows
open

and you see your poems
buried at birth
their blood still pounding

I watch you go under
ground under
pavement
under cathedrals and cafés
under the Seine
I feel you
looking
for access to
the sea
and I can only stand
there is no water here

Letter from a Sea Monster

you were not there when I
swam away   my arms and legs
growing longer with
each stroke until I
became the ocean
my body the waves
and the shore held
no call for me

every thousand years
you say   the sky is
red   and I come in the
summer   when the streams
have nearly lost their flow
I feel my limbs shrink
I stand uneasy
on your beach

you comfort me   you say
we will build together
and we make bread
and a house and
cloth and bowls
and when the rain begins
you stay under the roof

now the season of our touching
has passed   the rain runs
in serpent paths through
the earth   last night while

mist covered your sleep   I
lay on the wet sand
and stretched
and felt my body
lengthen again

To Gail from Cow's Cove

you carried your
two sleeping daughters
to the car then
headed north and
away from the
house on Highland Avenue
away and north
where the air would
be less heavy   where
it would be
easier to breathe   where
there were rumors of
women's land

now you struggle to
send out your report
a foreign correspondent
without a home paper

even the words for love and
war you must invent
reclaim from Hemingway
shape them to fit a
woman moving from post to
post   teacher   mother
lover   poet   holder-together
of fatherless children

remember   we met
searching for our

own vocabulary
ten years ago we were
startled at the
assignment   now we
know that it will
always be unfinished   that
for every word we
tend and nurture
others appear in the
popular slicks
dressed like whores

I receive your news
accounts of your
daughters' growing and
your students' learning
you write of dilemma
your lover's distance   the
haunting elusiveness of
women's land   and

the news under that   the
subterranean shifting   the
potential for unpredictable
power that sometimes
pushes against
whatever contains it   and
sometimes relaxes   appearing
calm as this cove
off a greater sea

Flight

every morning a woman stands
between two mailboxes in
front of the newsstand
Call me back   she
yells into the mailslot
pulling it open
slamming it shut   *Call*
me back   call me
I hear her before
I see the flowered
scarf knotted under her chin
her cry hovers like a gull
over the pounding rush
through the concourse under
Philadelphia   she
perches there as we
roll past   *Goddamn crackers*
fucking crumbs for supper
she plans to take off
this is rotten feeding ground
but she must hurry   already the
soot has collected heavily
on her skin   and the lack of
light and food causes
her head to nod   suddenly she
remembers an old flight path
she leans over the mailbox
flapping it open   shut   open   shut
until it lifts her out of there
calling to her lovers and children

waving good-bye   it is not until
later that the silence comes
when she finds herself
landed in the same spot
as though she had
never flown

White Trout

Long ago in Ireland a woman pined
for her lover who had been murdered
and thrown into a lake. As her sorrow
grew, the woman became thinner and
thinner. With her disappearance, the
villagers discovered a white trout, such
as no one had ever seen, swimming in
the lake.

grief attached itself to her
so that if she
buttered a scone or
put honey in her tea   it was
the grief that grew   it
was she who
continued each day to
wane   until
the villagers turned their
eyes from her
and when they looked again
she was gone

underground   maybe   they
thought   buried
when the moon was
full   but not by any
hand they knew   and
not a prayer or
chant they heard to
send her off   or

into air   maybe   they
thought   like a

frail saint taken
into heavy mist   to
hover over the fields and
linger a little even
if the sun grew hot

but she's not
here now   not part
of the talk   she's
cool   she's
smooth and silvery
she moves fast   cuts
a path wherever she
wants   she
leaps and dives   she
carries nothing on her
back   who

is this sleek white
fish   they ask   who
as though it were a
given   the spells and
changes   who
this grand trout   silver
or white as the sun and
moon move   and the
lake lies fresh and blue at
their feet   but she's

not greeting them   not
answering questions   she
slides and splashes and
rises and sinks   is

she looking for a
murdered love there
in the silt of the
lake   who knows if it's
so or not   she's
not saying

curiosity clings
scratches the skin   digs
in   until

enough   they say   it's
enough to see her at
sunrise or dusk   to
rest by the lake and
watch for her silver glint
it's enough that she's
here and
sacred   some say   as the
Fish of the Sign of
the Great Mother's Womb   it's
enough

some remember the
Celtic words for fountain and
lake   and walk to the
place where stones still
lie in the hills   and they
watch the lake   watch
her leap and
skim through the lake

you say it can't
end here   you say the
fishermen in New York
Japan and Spain speak

the same words as the
fisherman there on the
shore of a lake in
Kilarney   as though they
stand at the edge of
the same blue lake   as
though they link arms with
that fisherman   who

bored with his
usual catch   bored with his
usual   says   who

does this fish
think she is

no thought of
spells and changes
prayers and chants   he
flings those out as
he casts his net   and
gurgling up in his
throat   spurts a long
loud HA   that broad
guffaw you know

if he catches her   if
he spears her and
calls her supper   you
will know why the
trout carries circles of
blood on its side   if he

spears her again and
again   and she keeps on
swimming   you will

forget what
century it is   you will
wonder if the
spell proves true   does
the fisherman become a
minnow

the fins on the trout begin
to grow short
imperceptibly at first   as
the daylight in August

now no one has
seen that fish for sure
fish-woman headed toward
or away from the shore
woman-fish awaiting the
souls of the dead   to
swim with them   then
send them toward
shore again   no
one has seen that
fish for sure   or
woman emerge   but she's

part of the talk now   there
will be a

star   maybe   they
think   to mark her
rising   a
storm or brilliant flash
a stirring in the grass
restlessness in the
sheep and cows   there will
be something in

the air   maybe   they
think   something light in
the heavy mist that
hangs over the fields

so that when she
walks through the village
when she works in
her garden or
stirs honey in her tea
they will see her
they will know that
she's there

House by the Sea

"A house by the sea
is an honorable
goal in life"
   —Olga Broumas

the woman in
the Russian Tea Room
says I am not
goal-oriented   I have
nothing to do with
short distances and
straight lines   my
future is
watery   she tilts
the cup slightly
I want to say   look again
don't you see the house
the rough boards back
just enough from the surf
me   ankle-deep
my feet firm in
circles of water   my
eyes turned
straight ahead to
the great curve

About the Author

ALMITRA MARINO DAVID was born in Pittsburgh in 1941. She studied for a year at the University of Madrid, received a B.A. in Spanish from Dickinson College in 1963, and an M.A. from Kutztown University in 1974. She has taught Spanish, English as a second language, creative writing and women's studies. She currently teaches Spanish at Friends Select School in Philadelphia. Her poems and translations have been published in various journals; her chapbook, *Building the Cathedral*, was published in 1986 by Slash & Burn Press. *Between the Sea and Home* is her first book.

About the Cover Artist

ROCHELLE TONER was born in Des Moines, Iowa in 1940. She received a B.A. from the University of Northern Iowa, and M.A. and M.F.A. degrees from the University of Illinois. In 1972 she began teaching printmaking at the Tyler School of Art, Temple University, where she continues to teach and to serve as dean of the school. Her sculpture, prints, and drawings have been exhibited nationally and internationally. She is represented in numerous private and public collections including the Philadelphia Museum of Art. In 1992 her work was featured in *Printmaking: A Primary Form of Expression* by Eldon L. Cunningham. She lives with the author in Philadelphia. The cover art is water color on Arches cover paper.

About the Book

Marcia Barrentine designed the cover for *Between the Sea and Home*. She is a graphic designer and artist who lives in Portland, Oregon. The text typography was composed in Palatino. The cover typography was composed in Goudy Old Style. The book was printed on acid-free paper.

OTHER BOOKS FROM THE
EIGHTH MOUNTAIN PRESS

TRYING TO BE AN HONEST WOMAN
Judith Barrington

HISTORY AND GEOGRAPHY
Judith Barrington

AN INTIMATE WILDERNESS
LESBIAN WRITERS ON SEXUALITY
Judith Barrington, Editor

THE RIVERHOUSE STORIES
Andrea Carlisle

INCIDENTS INVOLVING MIRTH
Anna Livia

MINIMAX
Anna Livia

A FEW WORDS IN THE MOTHER TONGUE
POEMS SELECTED AND NEW (1971–1990)
Irena Klepfisz
Introduction by Adrienne Rich

DREAMS OF AN INSOMNIAC
JEWISH FEMINIST ESSAYS, SPEECHES AND DIATRIBES
Irena Klepfisz
Introduction by Evelyn Torton Beck

COWS AND HORSES
Barbara Wilson

A JOURNEY OF ONE'S OWN
UNCOMMON ADVICE FOR
THE INDEPENDENT WOMAN TRAVELER
Thalia Zepatos